T1-AWN-857

First Facts®

Transportation Zone

Fire Trucks in Action

by Anne E. Hanson

CAPSTONE PRESS
a capstone imprint

First Facts is published by Capstone Press,
151 Good Counsel Drive, P.O. Box 669, Mankato, Minnesota 56002.
www.capstonepub.com

Library of Congress Cataloging-in-Publication Data
Hanson, Anne E.
  Fire trucks in action / by Anne E. Hanson.
    p. cm. – (First facts. Transportation zone)
  Includes bibliographical references and index.
  ISBN 978-1-4296-6824-8 (library binding)
  1. Fire engines—Juvenile literature. 2. Fire extinction—Juvenile
literature. I. Title. II. Series.
  TH9372.H353 2012
  628.9'259—dc22   2011006033

Editorial Credits
Karen L. Daas and Brenda Haugen, editors; Gene Bentdahl, designer; Eric Gohl, media
    researcher; Laura Manthe, production specialist

Image Credits
Alamy/North Wind Picture Archives, 13; Sunpix, 10
BigStockPhoto.com/JK Studios, 5
Capstone Studio/Karon Dubke, 9, 22
iStockphoto/Dave Logan, 6; Eugene Kazimiarovich, 18
Library of Congress, 14, 17
Shutterstock/Kazela, 21; mikeledray, cover; Nathan DeMarse, 1

Printed in the United States of America in North Mankato, Minnesota.

032011   006110CGF11

Table of Contents

Fire Trucks

The siren wails. A loud
horn lets out a long honk.
You turn toward the sound
and see flashing lights.
Here comes a fire truck!
Firefighters drive these
trucks to the scene of a fire.
The trucks travel quickly.
Fire crews use the trucks to
put out fires.

Firefighters

Firefighters battle blazes. They rescue people from burning buildings and cars. They also help people who are hurt. Four to six firefighters ride on a fire truck. An **officer** leads the fire crews on the truck.

officer: someone who is in charge of other people

Parts of a Fire Truck

Firefighters ride in the truck's cab. The driver controls the truck with a steering wheel and brakes. Sirens, horns, and lights on the cab warn other drivers to move out of the way. A tank inside the truck holds water. Hoses are stacked near the top of the truck. The truck also carries ladders and other tools.

ladder

light bar

hoses

cab

water tank connection

MANKATO FIRE
PUBLIC SAFETY

PUBLIC
SAFETY

9

How a Fire Truck Works

An **engine** powers the fire truck and the water pump. After parking the truck, firefighters attach hoses. The driver flips a switch, and the engine starts pumping water.

engine: a machine that makes the power needed to move something

Bucket Brigades

Before fire trucks, people fought fires in bucket **brigades**. They formed two lines. One line passed buckets of water from a river or a well to the fire. The people at the end of the line threw water on the fire. The other line passed empty buckets back to the water source.

brigade: an organized group of workers

The First Fire Trucks

Pumps on carts served as the first fire trucks. People pulled a cart to a fire and powered the pump. The pump shot a stream of water through a pipe onto the fire. Some pumps had tanks. Others used water from a river or a well.

pump: a machine that forces water or foam through a hose

Early Fire Trucks

In the 1800s, horses pulled steam engines to fires. These engines used steam to pump water from a tank. People began to use motor-powered fire trucks in the early 1900s.

Fire Truck Rescue Today

    Fire trucks rush to emergencies. Some firefighters use hoses to shoot water into burning buildings. Other firefighters go into the buildings to help people. Firefighters provide medical care to those who are hurt.

Fire Truck Facts

- Some fire trucks are ladder trucks. Firefighters use these trucks to reach high places.

- Many firefighters live at the fire station when they are on duty. They cook meals and sleep there. They leave quickly when called to a fire.

- Dalmatian dogs are pets at some fire stations. These dogs ran next to early fire trucks. They kept rats and robbers away from the horses.

- Some fires cannot be put out with water. Firefighters spray foam on these fires.

- In the 1600s, children were firefighters too. They passed buckets in the bucket brigades.

Hands On: Check the Flow

Firefighters need a lot of water to put out a fire. Flow is the amount of water that runs through a fire hose. Fire crews need enough flow to put out the fire quickly. You can learn about flow.

What You Need

    garden hose
    a large plastic bucket

    a stopwatch or a watch with
      a second hand
    a friend

What You Do

1. Turn on the water at full force.
2. Fill the bucket with water. Have your friend empty the bucket when it is full. Do this for one minute. How many buckets can you fill?
3. Turn the water down. Repeat step 2.

You can fill the bucket faster when more water flows through the hose. Water flows through fire hoses at as much as 400 gallons (1,500 liters) per minute. Most fire trucks hold about 1,250 gallons (4,700 l) of water. They get more water from fire hydrants.

Glossary

brigade (bri-GAYD)—an organized group of workers

engine (EN-juhn)—a machine that makes the power needed to move something

foam (FOHM)—a mixture of bubbles used to put out fires

officer (OF-uh-sur)—someone who is in charge of other people

pump (PUHMP)—a machine that forces water or foam through a hose

Read More

Armentrout, David, and Patricia Armentrout. *The Fire Department*. Our Community. Vero Beach, Fla.: Rourke Pub., 2009.

Jango-Cohen, Judith. *Fire Trucks on the Move*. Vroom-Vroom. Minneapolis: Lerner Publications Group, 2010.

Lindeen, Mary. *Fire Trucks*. Mighty Machines. Minneapolis: Bellwether Media, 2007.

Internet Sites

FactHound offers a safe, fun way to find Internet sites related to this book. All of the sites on FactHound have been researched by our staff.

Here's all you do:

Visit *www.facthound.com*

Type in this code: 9781429668248

Super-cool stuff! Check out projects, games and lots more at
www.capstonekids.com

Index